VALLEY OF SHADOWS AND DREAMS

HIGHWAY 99   Atwater, California, 2008

VALLEY OF SHADOWS AND DREAMS

TEXT BY MELANIE LIGHT

PHOTOGRAPHS BY KEN LIGHT

Foreword by Thomas Steinbeck

Heyday, Berkeley, California

Library of Congress Cataloging-in-Publication Data

Light, Melanie, 1958-
 Valley of shadows and dreams / text by Melanie Light ; photographs by Ken Light ; foreword by Thomas Steinbeck.
    p. cm.
 Includes bibliographical references.
 ISBN 978-1-59714-172-7 (hbk. : alk. paper)
 1. Agricultural laborers--California--San Joaquin Valley. 2. Agricultural laborers--California--San Joaquin Valley--Pictorial works. 3. Agricultural industries--California--San Joaquin Valley. 4. Agricultural industries--California--San Joaquin Valley--Pictorial works. 5. San Joaquin Valley (Calif.)--Social conditions--21st century. 6. San Joaquin Valley (Calif.)--Social conditions--21st century--Pictorial works. 7. San Joaquin Valley (Calif.)--Economic conditions--21st century. 8. San Joaquin Valley (Calif.)--Economic conditions--21st century--Pictorial works. 9. San Joaquin Valley (Calif.)--Environmental conditions. 10. San Joaquin Valley (Calif.)--Environmental conditions--Pictorial works. I. Light, Ken. II. Title.
 HD1527.C2L54 2012
 331.7'63097948--dc23
                    2011030437
Cover: "Midnight," Fiesta Club, Tulare, California, 2007. Ken Light
Book design: Lorraine Rath

Orders, inquiries, and correspondence should be addressed to:
     Heyday
     P.O. Box 9145, Berkeley, CA 94709
     (510) 549-3564, Fax (510) 549-1889
     www.heydaybooks.com

Printed in Singapore by Imago

10   9   8   7   6   5   4   3   2   1

We dedicate this book to those in the valley who still live in the shadows but dream of justice

—ML & KL

VALLEY SKY Kerman, California, 2007

CONTENTS

WINTER ORCHARD Coalinga, California, 2011

Thomas Steinbeck

FOREWORD

As a lifelong student of history, I'm forced to agree with those social critics who state that there are few variations to the themes of hubris, greed, and violence that so often accompany the acquisition of wealth. Where that wealth is represented by thousands upon thousands of hectares of fertile farmland, ancient, medieval instincts for agrarian practices seem to come to the fore and prevail, especially in regard to the migratory battalions of field labor required to draw a profit from the land.

The arcane and often subtle traditions that key in on this kind of agricultural gluttony still prevail to this day. Sometimes the images in *Valley of Shadows and Dreams* may seem slightly obtuse to the uninitiated eye, but close examination of Ken and Melanie Light's exploration of California's Great Central Valley exposes a system and set of attitudes that go back to—and have changed little since—the region's conquest by colonial Spain. In one sense Ken and Melanie have managed something quite novel in this regard, for they have used the camera not just with an artistic sense of composition and social perspective, but also as a kind of archaeological tool of calibration that links past and present in the same image. The text handsomely laces these images into a cohesive portrait of the whole, while acknowledging that the saga is ongoing and still worthy of close attention.

In the empire-expanding year of 1513, the Spanish Crown financed Vasco Nuñez de Balboa to cross the Isthmus of Panama and lay claim to anything he found on the other side. Well, the enterprising little man found the Pacific Ocean, and in His Royal Majesty's name, he claimed the whole bloody ocean for Spain, as well as everything in it or on it, including long-populated eastern islands as yet unexplored by "civilized" Spain.

Now South America and Mexico are really big places, so it took a while, but with their sterling sense of cultural audacity, papally endorsed greed, moral amnesia, and profound tendency towards racial chauvinism, the Spanish ultimately conquered and subjugated every indigenous population they could lay their hands on, and in the process they systematically purloined everything of value that wasn't nailed down. And if perhaps they discovered something that they could neither steal nor destroy, they simply built a church on top of it.

The indigenous populations were totally overwhelmed, of course, and the ones who did manage to survive the bloodshed and disease were assimilated into the Spanish infrastructure as outright slaves owned by the state, or indentured servants wallowing in the numerous blessings afforded by the state-imposed church, which is essentially the same set of shackles in the scheme of things.

KEN AND MELANIE LIGHT'S EXPLORATION OF CALIFORNIA'S GREAT CENTRAL VALLEY EXPOSES A SYSTEM AND SET OF ATTITUDES THAT GO BACK TO—AND HAVE CHANGED LITTLE SINCE—THE REGION'S CONQUEST BY COLONIAL SPAIN.

From written records, and judging by all standards of any epoch, what the Spanish survey teams found was truly remarkable: rich alluvial and riparian deltas that had never known the bite of a plough, heavily timbered forests, mountain-bred rivers fat with salmon and beaver, and enough verdant grazing land to satisfy the gluttony of a thousand aristocratic Bourbon relatives.

Soon Alta California was neatly sliced up into a series of massive land grants that were parceled out to the richest of the king's subjects, with additional land and forced native labor gifted to the Church to support their extensive network of missions, and to maintain the King's Highway that connected them all together for the sake of rapid communication.

One would think that the effects of such complex and strenuous endeavors would be long-lasting and in the main relatively creative. But aside from the ubiquitous use of Spanish place names, and some very fine examples of eighteenth-century adobe architecture, the most enduring aspect of the Spanish colonial legacy was, and remains, a deep-seated racial and cultural bias. Unfortunately the disdain is directed towards most farm workers and a plethora of professions that might be more accurately termed "life-endangering labors." These mortal vocations have always been delegated to those people whose plight of reinforced poverty, usually based on "company" debt, kept the hapless farmhands culturally bonded to a socially curtailed and restricted education that would almost assuredly secure them to a life of the very same labors that had withered their parents, grandparents, and numerous generations before them.

Despite the fact that the vaunted conquerors of old have now melted away in all things save attitude and ambition, our modern traditions of agricultural and mine labor have remained remarkably feudal in dimension and effect. However, rather than suffer the indignity of being indentured to a titled overlord, field laborers are now theoretically indentured to the mega-corporations that own vast tracts of farmland, in America and elsewhere. In general, these are people who live and labor on the margins of poverty, and they are

DESPITE THE FACT THAT THE VAUNTED CONQUERORS OF OLD HAVE NOW MELTED AWAY IN ALL THINGS SAVE ATTITUDE AND AMBITION, OUR MODERN TRADITIONS OF AGRICULTURAL AND MINE LABOR HAVE REMAINED REMARKABLY FEUDAL IN DIMENSION AND EFFECT.

rarely adequately compensated for the chemical dangers and medical privations they habitually encounter while laboring to pick our crops or mine our coal.

A vast fertile area in northern California, known euphemistically as the Great Central Valley, proved to be one of those agricultural mother lodes that the Spanish discovered and chose to exploit to their fullest possible advantage. Though their efforts were rather modest by today's standards of agribusiness, the valley's development required the first large-scale relocation of indigenous, and therefore indentured, field labor in California.

Having spent some time as a reluctant combat photographer in Viet Nam, and then as a low-ranking photojournalist/stringer during two nerve-bending stints in Cambodia, Viet Nam, and Laos, I came to realize that despite the ragged adage equating the deceptive value of pictures and words, there were often soul-scorching incidents that could only be hinted at or defined with candid photographs; words would have failed, as they often do, to evoke the deep visceral truth that dwells beyond the grasp of intellect or logic alone. Indeed, I photographed the aftermath of scenes of combat that were so emotionally disturbing that I could only witness them through the viewfinder of my camera.

It is one thing to record the interactions of desperate people, violent or otherwise, against the backdrop of their conflict, but when the idiom involves the byzantine relationship between working people and the land to which they are inextricably bound—and which supposedly sustains them—balanced interpretation becomes a critical factor in fleshing out a complex and emotionally charged chronicle as honestly and as simply as the medium will allow.

As they did in Appalachia with their previous insightful volume, *Coal Hollow*, Ken and Melanie Light have now deftly chosen to document the Great Central Valley of California. They have accomplished this with the same impeccable focus upon detail, subject, and here, the almost spiritual influence of the fertile miles of verdant farmland that have remained an object lesson, if not a model of neofeudal greed and class-enforced poverty, for the past two hundred years.

Yet regardless of history, or our individual opinions, we would be well advised to view the portraits and landscapes in this book without a collateral reference to time. They illustrate in a nutshell the gist of all human history; "want" breeds "conquest," which in turn breeds "literal subjugation," "political castration," and "economic slavery." And all these elements are inextricably fused to the inevitable time bomb of cultural disorder, spiritual chaos, and economic devastation. Without correction, the whole mind-numbing process just winds itself up once more and becomes a self-perpetuating social mechanism that traditionally nurtures the seeds of its own destruction.

It was John Steinbeck's confirmed opinion that any culture that refused to protect and nurture those people who cultivated, harvested, and processed crops was playing long odds with potentially catastrophic starvation. To illustrate, he recalled that despite Sparta's vaunted military prowess and rigid self-discipline, when their helot slaves finally rebelled and refused to work their masters' fields, the Spartan state withered and reverted to barbarism—which wasn't really a radical step down for the Spartans, who had acquired their slaves using rather barbaric methods to begin with.

Thomas Steinbeck is a writer, a Vietnam war veteran and combat photographer, and the firstborn son of Nobel laureate John Steinbeck. He is the author of *In the Shadow of the Cypress* and *Down to a Soundless Sea*. He lives in California with his wife, Gail. His website is www.thomassteinbeck.com.

IT WAS JOHN STEINBECK'S CONFIRMED opinion that any culture that refused to protect and nurture those people who cultivated, harvested, and processed crops was playing long odds with potentially catastrophic starvation.

FOOD LINE Westside Community Center, Mendota, California, 2009

FIELD NOTES

"Men do change, and change comes like a little wind that ruffles the curtains at dawn, and it comes like the stealthy perfume of wildflowers hidden in the grass."

—John Steinbeck

When we began our exploration of California's Great Central Valley, it was surely not our intention to depict the agricultural industry as an exploitive abuser of unregulated capitalism. In our previous book, *Coal Hollow*, we set out to tell that very tale and to show that the injustices of the mining industry have still not been made right. What struck us about the valley initially was the contradictory impulses we saw in 2005 concerning the creation of residential developments on prime agricultural land. The struggle to understand that one aspect of life in the valley led us inexorably to the core of the power structure in the valley and how that group of people has coerced the state and federal governments to bend to their agenda.

The goal of this book is to use the region to illustrate how we citizens have allowed our democracy to become skewed. And yes, it might be inflammatory to many people in the valley. With *Coal Hollow*, there were a few West Virginians who felt they were being picked on by the publication of the book. When we explained what it was really about (no one in America should live in that kind of extreme poverty), they were on board. Most people from West Virginia were

grateful that we brought up this unfinished business and called the responsible parties to task. They felt it was important for the story they had lived to come out to the rest of the country; they felt their own experience had been validated, that wrongs should be righted.

As a nation we have been through some very tough times of late and it has become manifestly clear that the democratic process has been abused by powerful interests that control all the basics of our lives—food, money, and housing. The trickle-down effect of this—foreclosure, unemployment, and corn syrup–based diets—has gotten bad enough that it matters. Since we began the *Valley of Shadows and Dreams* project, our country has been through a cataclysmic chapter in which the curtain over the banking industry and monetary policy has been drawn aside. We now know that the process of democracy that we are taught in grade school was long ago cast aside in favor of sweetheart deals between congressmen and lobbyists. Government, as a concept and in practice, has been debased. But the reason government exists, especially the democratic varieties, is to check the ignoble bits of human nature: the will to excessive power, exploitation, fear, and greed. The struggle to maintain the balance between freedom and regulation occurs constantly and every generation must learn anew the lynchpins of that struggle and rein in the excesses.

When *The Grapes of Wrath* appeared in 1939, it created a national uproar. It was publicly banned, burned, and debated from coast to coast. Steinbeck was called a propagandist and socialist. In particular, the Associated Farmers of California called Steinbeck's description of horrific farm worker conditions "a pack of lies" and labeled it "communist." Nonetheless, Steinbeck was awarded the Nobel Prize for this novel in 1962 and it has become an iconic expression of American literature, required reading in high schools and colleges around the world. Similarly, when Upton Sinclair wrote *The Jungle*, an indictment of unregulated capitalism in the meatpacking industry, six publishers refused it. Doubleday finally published it, and when President Theodore Roosevelt read it, he was compelled to call for the investigation of the meatpacking industry which resulted in the Pure Food and Drug Act of 1906 and the Federal Meat Inspection Act of 1906.

Today, people are really angry and prepared to take action. They are angry at the bankers whose irresponsible behavior has cost so many their jobs and homes. It seems to us that people just need to know more about what is happening so they can find their own voice about this. People are ready to move forward and own this mess, the first step toward finding a new balance between those in power and the rest of us. There is a deep and broad need for independent information to circulate. This book is our attempt to add to that national debate. The story in the valley is parallel to the story in banking; the same kinds of relationships exist between Congress and agricultural industry groups. We sincerely believe the valley—and our nation—will never be a better place unless someone takes a stand and tells the unvarnished truth so that citizens can make good decisions about the direction of our nation. The American Dream is in our own hands. We must arm ourselves with real information and demand nothing less than real and intelligent reform.

If not for serendipity, this project might not have happened, even though this story and the valley are right in our backyard. One afternoon Melanie returned from a short trip through the valley to do some research on the *Life* magazine and social photographer Hansel Mieth. Hansel had done some of her earliest images in valley fields, in places like Huron and Buttonwillow, in the 1930s. Ken had become friends with Hansel in the late 1970s when she called him out of the blue. She had seen some of his early photos and told him they were kindred spirits in photography. Ken often visited her and talked about photography. In later years Melanie joined him. Because of this connection, a few years ago the Museum of Photographic Arts asked Melanie to write about Hansel for their show on pioneering women in photojournalism. In doing her research, Melanie drove into the region where Hansel had worked with her husband, Otto Hagel. She returned excited and maybe even a little agitated at what she had seen. The valley was undergoing massive changes. Booming housing developments were now spreading over once rich agricultural land, and she began to wonder who was buying these overpriced houses and how all this development would impact the workers, the air, the land, and California. She said, "This would be a great project for us. We should go and find out more," and we did.

The valley is a photographer's and writer's dream, an amazing mix of startling light and a kaleidoscope of faces and stories. Everywhere we turned during this project, people's stories pulled us in deeper, though their circumstances seemed to get more and more desperate the longer we worked. The project lasted five years, during which we witnessed the largest undocumented immigration march in Fresno history, the most massive foreclosures since the Great Depression,

THE VALLEY IS A PHOTOGRAPHER'S and writer's dream, an amazing mix of startling light and a kaleidoscope of faces and stories.

food lines, drought, the election of President Obama, valley boys dying as casualties of the war in Iraq, a huge citrus freeze that threw thousands of undocumented migrants out of work, and numerous other moments that Ken recorded with his camera and Melanie in her interviews and conversations.

We remember our first trip together into the valley, in 2006, cruising down Highway 5 at eighty miles per hour to Fresno for the May Day March, the first National Mobilization for Immigrant Workers' Rights. Tens of thousands of people poured into the streets of downtown Fresno. For many, it was the first time they'd put themselves so squarely in the public eye. They were standing up and saying, "We are part of the American Dream." It was as if they had been liberated from the shadows—a life where they feared that at any moment they might be stopped, questioned, and maybe deported. Always looking, always worrying, whether working in the fields or on construction sites building the new homes that were then popping up everywhere in the valley. We were struck by how much these workers love both America and Mexico, how much they believe in the American Dream: with the ability to move from field work to construction work, the dream seemed closer. People chanted "Sí, se puede" over and over until the excitement and exhilaration gave us headaches.

We walked among the people and saw an astonishing array of humanity. Melanie interviewed a very dignified and tall campesino standing at the curb. He had faded American and Mexican flags on a stick. He was dressed in all white, like someone from a photo from colonial California. He was a US citizen but spoke only Spanish, so Melanie spoke with him in her broken Spanish and he waxed on passionately about justice. On the sidewalk stood a tiny woman dressed all in white with a mantilla on her head, looking like a nun. Near her was a woman who has been a citizen for a long time. Her t-shirt had an iron-on picture of her son in military dress. He was serving in Iraq. She was a little acerbic but said she was proud of him, proud to be an American, and she wanted her family members who are not citizens to be able to work here and not be afraid. She wanted it to be easier

THE SHERIFF ADMITTED THAT HIS OWN HOME WAS UNDERWATER, WORTH LESS THAN WHAT HE HAD PAID FOR IT A FEW YEARS EARLIER. HE WAS STILL ABLE TO PAY HIS MORTGAGE, BUT HE SYMPATHIZED WITH THE PEOPLE WHO WOULD GET THESE NOTICES ON THEIR DOORS.

for them to become citizens. Three other tiny women hid behind a giant American flag while Ken was shooting them and one was quite shy, pulling the flag over her head.

We stopped for lunch at Fagan's Irish Pub, an obvious watering hole for city and state employees. It was a different universe; the usual hurried lunch scene seemed unaffected by the march. Melanie asked our blonde waitress if she was going over to see the march and she seemed not to know what we were talking about at first, then rolled her eyes and shook her head, "No, no, I won't be going to that." She paused as if to add something, then shook her head and laughed, walked away. Clearly, an entire stratum of valley people was not taking this march seriously and did not want to acknowledge this event. This bifurcated world intrigued us.

As we continued to explore the valley, the poverty and hardship of the workers and their families, amid such lush agricultural lands, was glaringly apparent. The first year we were in the field, a winter freeze destroyed the citrus crop, and we watched as people suffered. Their already hard lives of picking fruits and vegetables were abruptly interrupted as they lost the ability to support themselves. No money for food, for electricity, for rent. It was hard to witness.

We saw the subprime mortgage debacle hit the valley, one of the most impacted regions in the country. Ken watched and photographed as construction came to a halt. One afternoon he

> **THE DREAMS OF THESE WORKING PEOPLE** and immigrants had disintegrated into massive, undeveloped, empty sprawls. Acres of land with newly paved roads and newly installed streetlights and fire hydrants were now ghost towns, where tumbleweeds rolled down the silent streets.

accompanied the civil sheriff as he drove around posting foreclosure notices on homes. The sheriff admitted that his own home was underwater, worth less than what he had paid for it a few years earlier. He was still able to pay his mortgage, but he sympathized with the people who would get these notices on their doors—hardworking people whose dreams of owning a home were collapsing in foreclosure. Images of overgrown, uncared-for lawns and signs that told of bank ownership didn't adequately convey the enormity of what was happening. So one day Ken got the idea of hanging out at a local U-Haul truck lot in Merced to wait for a family that had been hit by the downturn, and he found one quickly: a couple with three children. As he photographed them, they told him how they had become homeowners for the first time and how quickly their new home had been taken from them by a system that seemed to be stacked against them. The dreams of these working people and immigrants had disintegrated into massive, undeveloped, empty sprawls. Acres of land with newly paved roads and newly installed streetlights and fire hydrants were now ghost towns, where tumbleweeds rolled down the silent streets.

Ken met many community activists as a result of the citrus freeze, and they introduced him to people in places like Tonyville and Plainview, communities that had been left behind and forgotten but were filled with stories crying to be heard. In particular, Francisco Barazza of Lindsay was an inspiring man who had worked hard and attained much.

He proudly showed Melanie the home he had bought and improved over the years and talked about his community work. He spoke about how he had spotted his wife, Irma, while in high school and how he had courted her; how they had worked in the fields and packing sheds and sold pots and pans door to door. Later, he took Melanie on a tour of his neighborhood, with the high school adjacent to orange groves that were sprayed with pesticide. He and Irma had tried unsuccessfully to bring attention to that issue. He then took Melanie to a new, recently abandoned development and they walked through the model homes together. It was very moving to see that this home with its Pottery Barn furniture and the gracious lifestyle implied by the accessories was the next, but perhaps unattainable, goal for him. Even after the bust, the prices on those homes were much too high.

One day while driving aimlessly, Ken saw from afar a multi-acre field that had been destined for development. It had a large, handsome sign advertising exclusive lots for luxury homes. The downturn meant that construction had been abandoned for the moment, if not forever. The land had once been a thriving walnut orchard. The developers had pulled out all the trees, save a ring of walnut trees left as ornamentation. Ken was curious, which required a stop to explore. A few cars were parked near the fringe of trees and some men, women, and a few children milled about. He walked slowly toward them so they could see his camera hanging around his neck. They seemed to realize Ken was not a threat and began to climb the trees and jump up and down on the thin branches. Walnuts dropped to the ground and those below scurried to pick up the nuts, gathering them into their aprons and then into large burlap bags. They were non-English-speaking gleaners scraping together a living by scavenging forgotten leftovers from the harvest. Ken watched in amazement as these families worked quickly, always looking over their shoulders, nervous that they might be discovered trespassing.

It was sobering to see not only how industrious people could be in times of need, but also that this remnant of a once-productive orchard had been transformed into nonfunctional eye candy where the walnuts would be a nuisance for the gardeners to sweep up and throw away. At least these trees provided support for these families, even at thirty cents a pound. This little luxury development, should it ever be completed, might be called "Walnut Gardens," the final insult to the land.

We got to know many people for whom securing adequate housing is a huge and constant struggle, while hundreds of homes lie vacant. We spent an afternoon at the Landrum Trailer Park in Mendota, which contains an entire universe. About thirty well-worn trailers stood too close to each other on the asphalt. They shimmered as the sun bounced off the asphalt yards, blistering the flat house paint off the plastic siding of the trailers. Most were occupied by extended families, but a few of the trailers were occupied by single men who came home from picking melons to play guitar and lose themselves in liquor. The tenants, nearly all from Michoacán, had painted the outsides of the trailers bright colors from a Mexican palette—turquoise, pink, green, indigo. Some families had lived here over ten years and their children had moved out, married, and moved into other trailers in this court. Power and water hookups, air conditioners, and homemade shrines to the Virgin were part and parcel of the gritty but extremely clean streetscape here. Aside from people, the only living things in this park were jumbles of flowers, weeds, and squash in occasional homemade planter boxes.

A group of children between eight and twelve played in the back of a pickup, a mix of cousins and friends. They were bored with summer, but they didn't like school either. They did chores—mopped and cleaned the dishes. They watched TV, but that was boring, too. Most of them said they were too old to play with toys and they just hung out now. The boys rode Sting-Ray bikes. They all cooled off with the hose. Their older brothers and sisters and their parents were just returning from a day picking melons in this cantaloupe center of the valley, while young stay-at-home mothers walked around on the blacktop with their babies in strollers. A group of men were delivered in a van. They were dressed up in straw cowboy hats, their best jeans, boots, and belts. They swung their duffle bags over their shoulders and it was clear they were returning from a trip to Mexico.

We met a Spanish-speaking family of seven that lived in a trailer the size of a bathroom. The mother sat in a crumpled heap in a lawn chair in the thirty inches between her trailer and her neighbor's, cutting beans. The head of the family, Sal, showed us his paycheck of $371 for two weeks of picking melons. Rent for the trailer is $300 each month. After the melon harvest he hoped to sign on with a labor contractor in other parts of the valley as different crops needed labor, but steady work is very difficult to maintain during the winter or when the harvests are poor.

Melanie interviewed Yolanda Prada. In her twenties, she lives with her mother, brother, and son. Next to the front door of their home, the family had built a crude shrine to the Virgin of Guadalupe. The front of the shrine was adorned with artificial flowers and apples. An overturned five-gallon bucket next to it served as a prayer seat. Yolanda let herself out of the trailer to speak with us, carefully closing the door so that we could not see inside. She told us her older brother was embarrassed and did not want us to see how poor they are. Though Yolanda is very friendly and open, she is not used to reflecting on her life, and the effort of pulling together fragments of

ONE NIGHT WE WENT TO A CANTINA WHERE A LARGE BRASS BAND BLEW THE ROOF OFF WITH THE SOUNDS OF MICHOACÁN. THE BEER FLOWED IN BUCKETS, AND HARD LIVES DISAPPEARED INTO A WILD PARTY OF DANCING AND THE FLASHING LIGHTS OF A DISCO BALL. COUPLES SLOW-DANCED, DRIFTING IN AND OUT OF THE BRIGHT, FOGGY LIGHTS, THEIR INTERTWINED BODIES ILLUMINATED FOR BRIEF SECONDS.

her world into a cohesive picture proved to be an emotional experience. As she realized how disparate her dreams were from her reality, a sense of defeat overcame her, flowing through her tears. Yolanda felt powerless, and we felt powerless, too, to help her.

Ken photographed industrial dairies where workers simply threw dead cows out on the street for weekly pickup, and he watched as workers with no protective gear sprayed pesticides from tractors, biplanes, and helicopters. He saw the results up close, in children and adults suffering from asthma and other health issues, and in communities like Kettleman City, where twenty babies were born with birth defects—oral deformities, such as cleft palates—in a fourteen-month period (three died). The plight of this impoverished community of fifteen hundred Spanish-speaking residents was, of course, ignored by local and state government agencies. The visit was heartbreaking.

The challenge of how to document water issues visually was a constant background noise in Ken's head—really more of a roar. One day while traveling through Modesto, he saw a huge sign:

"Waterfront Homes." The irony was not lost on him. Waterfront homes in a drought-stricken state, in a valley where farmers are up in arms over their decreased allotments of water? He stood there with his mouth wide open. After that, he began to notice empty reservoirs, irrigation ditches with tumbleweed—all manifestations of the lack of any sustainable or sensible water policy in the valley.

There were also wonderful moments of joy and happiness during our travels. The churches, where people praised the Lord and raised the rafters, were filled with love and hope. The community organizations worked hard to bring food and toys to the many posadas at Christmastime that resulted in smiles and giggles from the children. The valley produce, so rich and wonderful with flavor, delighted us wherever we went and we would bring back crates of peaches, apricots, and nectarines in the summer. One night we went to a cantina where a large brass band blew the roof off with the sounds of Michoacán. The beer flowed in buckets, and hard lives disappeared into a wild party of dancing and the flashing lights of a disco ball. Couples slow-danced, drifting in and out of the bright, foggy lights, their intertwined bodies illuminated for brief seconds.

The people we met generously opened their lives to Ken's camera and Melanie's microphone; they told us their stories, introduced us to others, and allowed us to enter their worlds, trusting us to faithfully portray them. Ken tried to look for and capture those moments—a gesture, a shaft of light illuminating a hand or a face—that illustrate the lives of ordinary people striving to preserve their humanity amid tremendous adversity. We hope that we have not failed them. Though Melanie had originally intended to let people's voices speak for themselves, telling such a complicated story in this way proved too much for a book with both photographs and text. There would not have been enough room to point clearly to why and how the valley has become such an extreme place. We wanted the reader to be able to walk away with some understanding of the underlying dynamics, so Melanie's words are directed to the left side of the brain and Ken's images speak to the right side.

The inspiration for *Valley of Shadows and Dreams* reaches back to Ken's earliest days as a photographer. In his twenties, first exploring the medium, he documented the agricultural fields of America. These images were published in two books in the early 1980s. The first had an introduction by Paul Taylor, Dorothea Lange's husband and partner, still in his office at UC Berkeley crowded with a life's worth of papers, articles, and memories of his efforts to help family farmers and migrant workers. His eyes would always light up when he talked about his lifelong passion for protecting the rights of others and about his belief that issues surrounding farm labor and water were not yet laid to rest. Ken's second book, *With These Hands*, had an introduction by César Chávez, who was still organizing farm workers at that time. Both of these men had large voices that resonated deeply with Ken. Paul's groundbreaking work with Dorothea proved that photography had a powerful and lasting voice, and César Chávez showed that the human spirit could rise powerfully to fight injustice. The photographs in *Valley of Shadows and Dreams* close an artistic circuit that began thirty or so years ago; Ken hopes this vision is a deeper and more mature one.

Ken's subsequent photographic journeys chronicling the underclass of America often took him far from our home in the Bay Area. This project in our backyard forced us both to reexamine our lives in California. Like so many of our fellow Californians, we haven't really thought about the communities and people that provide our food, or the labor that has made the state what it is for quite some time. It's easy for the valley to be invisible to those of us who live in the big coastal cities.

If you look behind the fantasy of the California Dream, so carefully crafted, you will see there are shadows, too. The Great Central Valley has provided the dream for many, but it is deeply shadowed. We hope that this record and text about the land and its people will plainly show what the lack of visionary thinking on the part of our politicians and leaders has wrought. Our sincerest wish is that this book will bring readers closer to the truth and inspire everyone to look, see, and act—so much is at stake.

SIGN WITH BULLETS   California Aqueduct, Modesto, California, 2008

Melanie Light

VALLEY ON THE VERGE

The brand-new Ford F-150 rolled to a stop on the gravel levee next to the San Joaquin River. The driver, Rick Cosyns, was nearly at the end of a tour of his twenty-five-hundred-acre farm of wine grapes, alfalfa, and almonds. Earlier, we stood over the roar of his underground reservoir of water as he tipped his straw cowboy hat back and smiled. "That's a beautiful sound." At the corner convenience store at the crossroads of vast, flat tracts of farmland, he nodded to the field workers, who respectfully and deferentially called him "jefe." He lovingly described each gargantuan piece of machinery in his shed. He explained how a laser-flattened field is tilled by satellite navigation. After setting the coordinates, the driver has only to decide which Mexican radio station he wants to listen to. The machine will dig; place pesticide, specially coated seeds, and fertilizer; cover it all up; and turn at the end of the row all by itself.

He bounced a huge drum of Paraquat from the back of his truck onto a tire and declared himself a steward of the land. He would never do anything to harm it and wished the government would just stop regulating his business. He breathed in the air deeply, demonstrating his own belief in the goodness of his land. "There is nothing wrong with the air. It wouldn't be polluted at all except the smog that the Bay Area sends over into the valley." We drove past an organic farm, and he told me how labor-intensive it is to grow organically. "You cannot farm almonds organically." I asked what he meant, thinking

he didn't want to spend the three years required to convert. "You can't." End of conversation.

Now, as we were riding high on the levee, an almond orchard fanned out on one side of the road, and the river flowed through a canal on the other. The truck startled a killdeer. It flitted about twenty feet away, dancing and flapping its wing and making its namesake call, "killdeer, killdeer." Rick explained that it was cleverly pretending that its wing was broken, to entice us away from its eggs. We got out and I could see the truck tires had rolled to a stop very close to the eggs, which look exactly like large chunks of gravel.

Growers, ranchers, and even beyond that, the corporate giants holding the purse strings in Washington are all flapping their wings, calling out, "We are stewards of the earth," or "Climate regulation deadlines are impossible to meet" while the two-ton truck of ecological and social disaster is about to roll right over all of us.

I.

Despite having lived in California nearly my entire life, I am an outsider to the inner workings of the Central Valley's people, culture, and economy. Like most coastal Californians, I travel through the valley at breakneck speed on the way to Tahoe or Los Angeles, enduring the hours of monotonous, flat land lined with miles and miles of trees, or a blurred green that nonfarming people relegate to "nothingness."

1

In the early eighties I had the opportunity to fly from Oakland to Harris Ranch. As we passed over the East Bay hills into the valley proper, I was shocked that the uncultivated perimeter of the Great Central Valley was desert. The contrast of the vast, uniformly green fields and orchards against the scrubby brown land looked like a grade-school collage. The fields were flat squares, possibly several miles long, and from time to time small clumps of buildings would pop up. I guessed them to be small towns. The entire valley before me, which is about the size of Tennessee, had been completely engineered to accommodate industrial farming and population growth far to the south. Except for the perimeter, every single living thing had been placed where someone planned it to be and had shaped it just so. A fake, cement river ran right down the middle, taking water from the north down to faucets and swimming pools in Los Angeles and San Diego. It was like a farmer's theme park, but there was nothing trivial about its impact: the 81,500 farms and ranches pull in $36 billion annually for over four hundred commodities, making California the number one state for farm revenue and representing 11.2 percent of total US farm revenue. California produces nearly half of US-grown fruits, nuts, and vegetables and is the country's largest dairy producer.[1] The number two state is Texas, which has under $20 billion in cash receipts.[2]

As the plane approached the landing strip at Harris Ranch, the smell and sight of hundreds of cows standing knee-high in mud and manure in the largest feedlot on the West Coast came into view. By car, "Cowschwitz," as many call it, marks the halfway point between San Francisco and Los Angeles. It is a stretch of road where all drivers acquire a lead foot and roll up their windows until they pass the ranch of one hundred thousand cows. This feedlot, where several hundred cows wait to be shipped off and butchered for In-N-Out each day, is next to the restaurant in which families merrily order up steak and enjoy themselves at the Harris resort. Is there a profound

disconnect between us and where our food comes from, or is this a healthy expression of a carnivorous society?

This brief encounter with the Great Central Valley and modern farming rolled to a dusty corner of my mind, where a strange sort of denial persisted. I preferred to think of the "Happy Cows" campaign developed by the California Milk Advisory Board: "Great cheese comes from happy cows. Happy cows come from California."

In 2005 I traveled into the valley to do research on an activist photographer, Hansel Mieth, who had documented the lettuce strikes in the thirties. I scrolled through hundreds of microfiche newspaper articles in the Tulare County Library that documented the cotton strike of 1933. Then I went to the county courthouse in Visalia to look through the death reports. The clerk handed me large tomes with line after line of loopy, old-fashioned handwriting in faded ink from the fountain pen. The names of hundreds of men, women, and children who had lived and died in the valley clawed at my curiosity. Who were these people with names of every ethnic origin? What was the fabric of their lives? That inspired me to turn off the well-worn Highway 99 and travel through farm towns—places like Chowchilla, Biola, and Hanford.

As I drove now, my senses more attuned to the people and landscape after having immersed myself in some of the local history, I saw the same thing happening all over the valley. The fruit bowl of America was being planted with its final crop: ticky-tacky cookie-cutter houses and gated communities with waterfront homes on man-made lakes. As I drove home into the sunset, the two lanes of traffic driving back into the valley were bumper to bumper for miles and miles. I started to notice that there were literally hundreds of subdivisions going in and almost as many for-sale signs on agricultural land. According to the Great Valley Center, nearly 28 percent of land in the Central Valley converted to urban use between 2000 and 2006 was prime farmland. That amounted to 35,488 acres of land originally home to native peoples, grasses, oaks, and tule elk. Subsequently razed and sown to feed millions of people all over the globe, this land has now been transformed to the least efficient kind of residential development known. And once land is paved over to create dams and housing, it is highly unlikely to see the light of day again.

There are numerous motivations for farmers to sell their land. Family farms have their own set of pressures: estate settlements at the turn of a generation; accumulation of debt; a younger generation's loss of interest in farming. Fragmented ownership can make farming too difficult. By the third generation the landowners are no longer farmers, and farmers are no longer landowners: distant owners are leasing out their land to be farmed, and they are simply not connected to the land in the same way. Sometimes an orchard has run its course and needs to be replanted, and an old orchard is worth more as a development plot than as agricultural land. The land can be fatigued and suffer from the buildup of salt in the soil; access to and affordability of water is an increasingly important factor. Another significant issue is the constant bickering between farmers on the fringe of developed land. Even with Right-to-Farm ordinances in place, which protect farms from new regulations and lawsuits against the noise and odors they generate, these tensions, plus the lure of money offered by developers, are often enough to push farmers into selling their land. As Eric Hvolboll, a Santa Barbara County avocado farmer and eighth-generation Californian, puts it, "There are not many farmers so invested in their work that they can justify the opportunity cost of not selling...Why risk your life, doing a dangerous job, working sixty hours a week, when you could make more money doing nothing?"[3]

A walk through the newly developed model homes is almost irresistible. The homey tableaus describe a life full of new things and a future that will only get better. Suddenly I am picturing my family sitting at the granite kitchen bar top discussing our day as I pull out snacks from the stainless steel refrigerator. Then I go back outside to the arid, flat, industrial farmland that abuts the development and spreads out to the horizon. I ask the model home representatives,

I SAW THE SAME THING HAPPENING all over the valley. The fruit bowl of America was being planted with its final crop: ticky-tacky cookie-cutter houses and gated communities with waterfront homes on man-made lakes.

shopkeepers, and realtors, "Who is going to buy these homes?" Given that the primary businesses are agriculture, landfills, and prisons, how would a $35,000 annual salary pay for a $400,000 home? Heads shake and people mumble, "Commuters and retirees."

Community leaders and investors in the valley saw opportunity in California's expected population explosion—23.5 million more people between 1995 and 2040—to turn a low-income region with minimal urban infrastructure into a region that would attract and retain highly educated people who have disposable income. And the valley could use a boost: the region still has one of the state's highest unemployment rates, due to the sporadic nature of farm work, and the lowest-paying jobs in California. The idea was to create jobs by building, which would attract businesses like Walmart, which would, in turn, attract workers and businesses requiring more complex skills and so on, until the region was diversified and prosperous. That logic gave rise to participation in Ponzi-like development that began to collapse in 2006.

Now, after the subprime mortgage debacle has unfolded, these homes arrayed across former farmland have created new problems in this region. People lost their homes in unfathomable numbers, and migrant and undocumented workers who had moved from the fields to better paying construction jobs found themselves without work as building came to a standstill and a three-year drought minimized agricultural work. There is no money or credit available to address the ongoing lack of affordable housing. In addition to the huge loss of revenue from lower property taxes, more budget strain has resulted as developers declare bankruptcy and miss payments to cities. It is a downward spiral: lower housing values lead to lower tax revenue, which leads to even fewer services. Residents struggle to find affordable housing in trailers, apartments, and even cars, while hundreds of new homes lie vacant, deteriorating in the hot valley sun. Squatters and vandals invade these properties and use them as a base for the thriving drug economy in the valley, making them much less attractive as salable units.

As I stand in the middle of this landscape, a certain line of logic begins to form in my mind. It is all-important for a country to be able to feed itself. We know that the population will only grow, requiring more food be produced. We also know that our supply of land will not grow, and may, in fact, decrease with global warming. Doesn't it stand to reason that there should be some sort of master plan, or at least some kind of national policy that would attempt to recognize and balance these pressures? Who is in charge here?

RESIDENTS STRUGGLE TO FIND affordable housing in trailers, apartments, and even cars, while hundreds of new homes lie vacant, deteriorating in the hot valley sun.

LAND   Stanislaus County, California, 2008

NEW HOMES AND AGRICULTURAL LAND Tulare County, California, 2008

TULE FOG   San Joaquin River, Madera County, California, 2009

ROPE SWING, 6 P.M., 100°F   San Joaquin River, California, 2010

BILLBOARD, PHEASANT RUN GOLF COURSE   Highway 99, Chowchilla, California, 2009

12

VALLEY FIELDS Tulare County, California, 2008

TRACTORED, AVENUE 368   Traver, California, 2007

"+/- 129 ACRES" Chowchilla, California, 2009

CARMEN, 18 YEARS OLD, 7 MONTHS PREGNANT, AND GUADALUPE   Tulare County, California, 2007

DRYING ALFALFA, HIGHWAY 180 Central Valley, California, 2006

DAIRY #2 Lindsay, California, 2007

MINI-MART WITH WWII FLIGHT TRAINER Old Highway 41, Caruthers, California, 2010

"HAVE A PEPSI" HIGHWAY 41 CAFÉ Lemoore, California, 2007

INTERSTATE 5 Tulare County, California, 2008

DROUGHT, FARM RESERVOIR King County, California, 2007

DOWNTOWN Mendota, California, 2008

"NEW HOMES" Fresno County, California, 2009

"ONLY GOD CAN JUDGE ME" Drive-in, Madera County, California, 2007

LANA, 55 YEARS OLD, 9 MONTHS HOMELESS Taco Flats Hooverville, Fresno, California, 2009

"IN LOVING MEMORY OF SAL GALVAN" Roadside memorial, Herndon, California, 2008

DEVELOPMENT South Lake Tahoe Drive, Chowchilla, California, 2008

CALIFORNIA AQUEDUCT Tulare County, California, 2008

HOUSE AND DOLL Firebaugh, California, 2009

DESERTED SUBDIVISION Atwater, California, 2009

WALNUT GLEANERS, 30¢ A POUND El Rio Estates, Visalia, California, 2008

NEW DEVELOPMENT Fresno County, California, 2007

FIELD WORKERS Tulare, California, 2008

"LAKE FRONT HOMES" Bella Lago master plan community, Manteca, California, 2008

"STOP THE CONGRESS CREATED DUST BOWL" Huron, California, 2010

II.

As far as I can tell, our free-market policy precludes a carefully thought-out plan for the valley. It seems as though the valley's politics and economics have been shaped by parochial and short-term profit-making values and practices. Local and state governments have focused on the special interests of landowners since the rough riders who settled California figured out, very early in the game, that whoever controlled the water controlled the economy of California.

Above all other issues, the management of water illustrates how a valuable resource which should be under the management of the state is de facto largely controlled by a small group of people invested in agricultural interests. The constitution of California hews to the public trust doctrine regarding water. In 1983 that provision was expanded to include all water in California. In plain English, that means that all California citizens own all the water in California. Yet a small number of landowners, largely in the valley, managed to aggregate massive water rights early on in the settlement of the state. Settlers moving across the New World from east to west determined riparian water rights by the same method that had been in place since medieval times: whoever owns the land next to the river owns the water that crosses there. The compulsion to conquer the mighty

rivers that flow from the Sierra into the Great Central Valley began in 1876 with the very first dam and irrigation canal built across the Kings River by a partnership between William Sanders and Moses Church, which defied the doctrine of public trust and defined a model for acquiring water in California. This dam and canal system were built through appropriation, legally termed "first in time, first in right," but which might as well be called "might over right" because whoever gets access to use the water has precedence over anyone downstream. Forever.

Water that is secured through pumping the aquifer is not regulated at all. Growers have pumped the valley's aquifer so hard and so fast over the past sixty years that parts of the land have collapsed. Yet due to labyrinthine water laws and bizarre management practices, brand-new housing developments are built around man-made recreational lakes out of which thirty-foot-high fountains spray water into the dry air. They are truly worried about getting enough water, and so are looking increasingly to the mountains for their water sources. For example, the Westlands Irrigation District is the largest water district in the US. The district is located in Fresno and Kings County and needs more water for its six hundred thousand acres. Its yearly allotment of water is regulated by the federal government, and it has been significantly reduced over the past few years. The managers have their eyes set on Shasta Dam, located three hundred miles away. The plan is to acquire the water rights to land upstream from the dam and lobby to raise the dam, so water would be backed up and stored on their newly acquired land. They would then, effectively, "own" that water. To do that they have bought three thousand acres of the Hills family's Bollibokka Club for $35 million. This land lies along the river that feeds into the dam. If and when the federal government raises the dam, Westlands will sell their riverfront land to the government to be flooded, but will retain water rights. Then they will attempt to siphon off that water to their fields in the desert via a new peripheral canal, which they will lobby the government to build as well.

The belief that more dams will provide enough water is fixed in the minds of the growers in the valley despite much evidence and experience to the contrary. Dams have not lived up to their promise. They are an ecological hazard, cause flooding, and have been linked to earthquakes. Reservoirs only last as long as it takes them to fill with silt. Gradually, the capacity of a dam is reduced until the silt must be removed. Unfortunately, the process for the removal of silt is generally not designed into the plans for new dam.[4] Nonetheless, every farmer, rancher, and grower I spoke with is zealously in favor of more dams in California.

ANOTHER EGREGIOUS, ENDEMIC injustice of the valley is exposed: the long-term struggles of farm workers to make a living wage.

The Westlands Water District has the power and the savvy to make its plan a reality—whether or not it's good for any concerned party. In April of 2009 the district partnered with the California Latino Water Coalition to hire the publicity firm Burson-Marsteller to design a "Water March." The client roster of this firm includes Blackwater USA, the Nigerian government, and Philip Morris. The strategy was to put a "human face" on the water crisis precipitated by the drought of 2007–2009, to convince the public that actions like building and raising dams and siphoning water from the Delta are ultimately humanitarian. Spanish-speaking workers, many undocumented, were hired to march and carry signs that they could not understand. The speeches focused on the high rate of unemployment and the great desire of the farmers to keep their workers employed so they wouldn't have to stand in food lines. The organizers fed the press their carefully crafted statements about how outsiders and environmentalists care more about some species of endangered fish than feeding humans. That is what we read with our morning coffee. While they make plans behind the scenes to achieve their goals, Westlands is creating a story for the public that will garner sympathy at the polls. Ultimately, whether or not they have the public's support, they have the ways and means to get the Shasta Dam raised and other dams built.

What outsiders don't understand is that the drought didn't create this state of affairs among farm workers. A chronic 30 percent unemployment rate is normal for agricultural workers, and food giveaways have been a normal part of valley life for at least fifteen years. When the backstory is fully unpacked, not only is the specious argument about water use revealed, but another egregious, endemic injustice of the valley is exposed: the long-term struggles of farm workers to make a living wage.

Another dynamic that outsiders do not know is that a great deal of the Westlands Water District's land has been rendered unusable by the buildup of salt from years of irrigation. Water imported from the mountains in California has high levels of salts, such as selenium, which cannot drain properly through the layer of clay that lies beneath the valley floor. Up to 30 percent of the land has been slated for retirement. Landowners have several options for dealing with this vexing problem, but the fact is, farming itself diminishes available farmland. How major infrastructure projects are created, and how complex policies for life-sustaining elements like water are determined should not be left to this self-serving community. These issues define and shape all of our lives.

III.

There is no doubt that California landowners have created a huge, multinational business. In 2009 about 1.6 million migrant, mostly undocumented and seasonal farm workers planted, grew, and picked crops valued at $34.8 billion, a staggering amount of food, especially given that the average worker's annual income is $15,000; about 45 percent of them do not have enough food to eat; and farm work has been designated the third-most dangerous occupation in our nation.[5]

Growers enjoy numerous benefits and special treatment from the government while the vast majority of their workers do not even enjoy the basic human rights of citizenship. It is true that farming is at the mercy of the weather and the interplay between world events and economies. Good people do lose their farms for tragic reasons. But those people tend to have small farms that carry more risk than the larger farms, and benefits are not determined proportionate to risk. Here are just a few examples of this chasm, of how rights and benefits stack up for the owners while workers are cut out of the system.

In 2007, during the horrible citrus freeze in the valley, there was hardly any work in the fields and people were worried about where their next meal might materialize. Farmers were paying workers one dollar per tree to knock off all the damaged oranges. They could clean off about twenty trees a day. Just lunch costs five dollars, never

GROWERS ENJOY NUMEROUS BENEFITS AND SPECIAL TREATMENT FROM THE GOVERNMENT WHILE THE VAST MAJORITY OF THEIR WORKERS DO NOT EVEN ENJOY THE BASIC HUMAN RIGHTS OF CITIZENSHIP.

mind gas, rent, bottled drinking water, and providing for a family. The farmers have crop insurance and government money. Most field workers have nothing because they are not citizens or regular employees. Even the free food handouts that churches, cities, and various groups coordinate on a regular basis are only supposed to go to citizens. Yet in that same year, $5 billion in subsidies were given to farmers, whether they needed it or not, and five of the top twenty recipients were in California: Sandridge Partners ($1.06 million); District 108 Farms ($730,000); Dublin Farms ($626,000); Colusa Indian Community Council ($483,000); and R Gorrill Ranch Enterprises ($419,000). Very few California farms received subsidies for conservation.[6]

In California, farmers have a way to sidestep property taxes. The Williamson Act, created forty-five years ago, protects agriculture and grazing land from urban sprawl. Under the act, local governments enter into ten-year contracts with landowners who promise to keep their land undeveloped in return for property tax breaks. Today about half of California's farmland—16.6 million acres—is under Williamson Act contracts, which cover many billions of dollars in crops and scores of commodities, from wine grapes to walnuts.[7] Presumably, this protection helps to ensure our continued ability to feed ourselves and preserve smaller farms near urban areas, but it's highly problematic in concert with other government and economic policies: this tax break not only has reduced income for the state but is a burden on the valley's school districts. Not only does 21 percent of a school district's budget come from local property tax, but when land is developed, fees levied for development go to schools. To remedy the loss of local property taxes, California pays out $38 million in "backfill" each year to counties. That is another indirect food cost. Nonfarmers are paying the property taxes for farmers and losing allocations for their own towns to fund the towns around farms. Despite the near-bankrupt state budget, 85 percent of the backfill was scraped together in 2010 for farming counties because the government believes the Williamson Act program is so important.

Growers buy water at a fraction of the cost that everyone else pays. That privilege is not burdened with any responsibility to conserve water for the rest of the state or to control the use of water so that the quality remains high. To wit, growers have pumped groundwater so severely over the past decades that many residents who live in the valley must either drink water with significant levels of arsenic or buy bottled water.

While some farm workers do move into a viable working-class lifestyle, obtain citizenship, and realize their dream of owning their own land, the uphill trek is formidable. It is truly hard to imagine the poverty in the valley, parts of which are now number one in the nation for density of poverty. Recent reports have called the region "worse than Appalachia," with half of the valley's residents having

annual incomes below $16,746. This is where the state school test scores are the lowest, 50 percent of the children have asthma, and multiple families live together in substandard housing.

This culture did not develop entirely by accident. Mark Arax and Rick Wartzman tell how the agricultural industry evolved in their pioneering book, *The King of California*. Farmers from the Deep South came to start fresh after boll weevils had destroyed the cotton industry at the beginning of the twentieth century. Cotton farmers like J. G. Boswell sought to reincarnate their plantations in California and even imported their black workers at first. They moved on to hire the local brown-skinned workers from Mexico, and many other immigrant groups have served time working the valley floor. In some very real way, the Great Central Valley is still deeply southern in its culture.

Paul Taylor and Dorothea Lange studied the migration of ruined tenant farmers into California and the West. Their *American Exodus* was published in 1939 and was the basis for hearings in the US Senate on civil liberties violations against farm workers. Although the government established minimum requirements for working conditions for agricultural workers, their lot was only marginally improved: the Fair Labor Standards Act (FSLA) of 1938 had exempted agricultural workers. If you were a steelworker, a coal miner, a janitor, or a waitress, the FSLA would protect you. While every other worker in the United States was guaranteed a minimum wage, overtime, and

IN SOME VERY REAL WAY, the Great Central Valley is still deeply southern in its culture.

other rights, agricultural workers had no rights at all. The minimum working age of sixteen was established, but the minimum age in agriculture is fourteen years old. Children as young as ten or eleven may work as hand-harvest laborers for up to eight weeks in a year with the consent of a parent or guardian.

That inequality of rights has its roots in the Jim Crow era. As a *New York Times* editorial explained in 2009, "Segregationist Southern Democrats in Congress could not abide giving African-Americans, who then made up most of the farm and domestic labor force, an equal footing in the workplace with whites. President Roosevelt's compromise simply wrote workers in those industries out of the New Deal. They were thus sidelined from the labor movement, with predictable results. Though the Dixiecrats have all long since died or repented, the injustice they spawned has never been corrected."[8]

It was not until 1966 that the efforts of César Chávez and Dolores Huerta and the United Farm Workers resulted in amending the FSLA to include some farm workers. And finally, in 1982, more protections were given to farm workers through the Migrant and Seasonal Agricultural Worker Protection Act, though farm workers are still not legally entitled to overtime pay.

In 1986 it became illegal to hire undocumented workers. In spite of this, today over half of California's agricultural labor force is classified as "foreign-born noncitizens."[9] All workers, including undocumented workers, theoretically, have the same labor rights. Yet the industry operates as if farm workers were still unprotected by labor law. Farm workers themselves often do not know their rights and nearly three-quarters of undocumented workers do not know they have any rights at all or how to pursue them. The fear of deportation,

for the undocumented workers, and of "blacklisting," for the citizen workers, prevents them from reporting abuses.

The courts are rife with cases of extreme abuse as outlined in "Weeding Out Abuses," a 2010 report by Oxfam America and Farmworker Justice, including numerous cases of slavery that were prosecuted between 1997 and 2010 across the nation in which labor contractors kept farm workers in indentured servitude and physically abused them. In addition to shorting paychecks and charging extra for transportation in illegal trucks, crew leaders routinely deny workers clean water and safe, licensed housing. There is so much sexual harassment that the lettuce fields of some Salinas growers are called "fields of panties." The Department of Labor does not keep track of how often it finds repeat or willful violations or whether or not penalties were imposed for the violations. These are the invisible workers of our nation.

Agricultural lobbyists—the National Council of Agricultural Employers, the American Farm Bureau Federation, state farm bureaus, the California Grape and Tree Fruit League, and others—have attempted to weaken federal and state labor laws. Such groups make various arguments, including that compliance is onerous, that the law "unfairly singles out agriculture," that the enforcement of the law is heavy-handed, and that they are "competing in a global economy where many countries have even fewer protections for workers."[10] What does that mean? Does that mean it is too expensive to give our agricultural laborers rights that workers in other industries enjoy? That US farmers will not profit if they have to pay a living wage and offer safe working environments? If that is true, modern agriculture is an inhumane and unacceptable practice.

DUST San Joaquin County, California, 2008

FIELDS Tulare County, California, 2008

LAWN SPRINKLER, 11:30 A.M. New subdivision, Newman, California, 2008

TUMBLEWEED Laguna Canal CK 109.10, Central California Irrigation District, Firebaugh, California, 2009

DROUGHT, EMPTY RESERVOIR, WINTER Chowchilla, California, 2009

WATER MARCH Highway 33, Mendota, California, 2009

"WE NEED WATER 4 JOBS" Airplane, Water March, Firebaugh, California, 2009

TULARE LAKE, EXTINCT FRESHWATER LAKE, ONCE THE LARGEST FRESHWATER LAKE IN THE WEST Tulare County, California, 2008

ASPARAGUS PICKER, Madera County, California, 2007

TREE NO. 30 Lindsay, California, 2006

COMMERCIAL BEEKEEPERS Madera County, California, 2006

BURNING FIELD Tulare County, California, 2007

IMMIGRATION DEMONSTRATION, May Day, Fresno County, California, 2006

INAUGURATION OF BARACK OBAMA   01.20.2008 9 a.m., Modesto, California, 2009

FUNERAL OF CORPORAL NATHAN HUBBARD Killed in action, Iraq, Clovis, California, 2007

"EN MEMORIA OF OSBALDO OROZCO" Killed in action, Iraq, Rosario (Osbaldo's aunt) and Danny, Earlimart, California, 2008

IMMIGRATION DEMONSTRATION May Day, Fresno County, California, 2006

QUINCEAÑERA Tranquility, California, 2006

CHILDREN ON PORCH Plainview, California, 2006

ALEXIS Christmas, Plainview, California, 2006

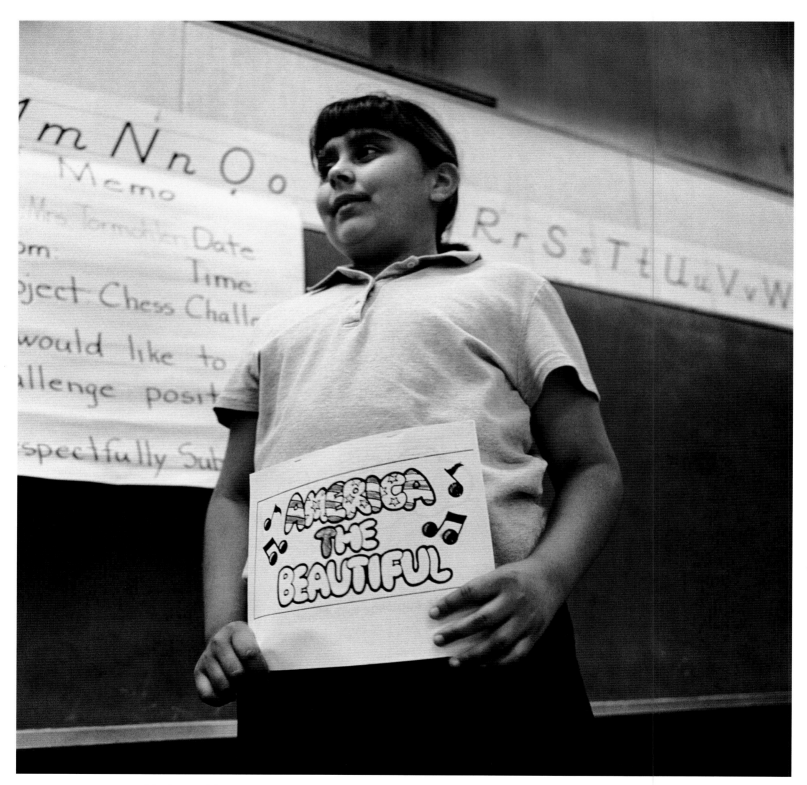

"AMERICA THE BEAUTIFUL" Mrs. Bowman's 2nd grade class, Farmersville, California, 2007

ELEMENTARY SCHOOL, GRADES 2–3 66 percent English-as-a-second-language (ESL), Farmersville, California, 2007

JOE, 33 YEARS OLD, UNEMPLOYED FARM WORKER Trailer court, Firebaugh, California, 2009

74

BARBERSHOP Merced, California, 2007

THE SCREAM Halloween, Plainview, California, 2007

JOSE, 34 YEARS OLD Homeless encampment, Fresno, California, 2009

"NO CERVEZA" Public park, Le Grand, California, 2009

"BEER" Strathmore, California, 2008

SATURDAY AFTERNOON Mendota, California, 2006

MIDNIGHT Fiesta Club, Tulare, California, 2007

AMERICAN FLAG Highway 33, California, 2007

IV.

Another contentious issue has to do with the government subsidies that US and European farmers receive, which artificially drive down the cost of their products. Because wealthy countries can afford domestic subsidies, critics argue that they promote poverty in developing countries by artificially driving down world crop prices to the point where it is cheaper for poor countries, which cannot subsidize the production of food, to buy food from the US and Europe. The result is that developing countries become dependent on food from wealthy countries. Farmers, instead of improving the agricultural and economic self-sufficiency of their home countries, are instead forced out of the market and perhaps even off their land.

There is no more stark example of this than the story of the federal cotton subsidy. Cotton used to be the biggest crop in California, at one time covering 1.6 million acres. In 2010 only about 300,000 acres were planted with cotton, because the tight supply of water has reduced the feasibility of that crop.[11] California is now second in the nation, after Texas, which produces about 600,000 acres of cotton. Nonetheless, in California, according to Kari Hamerschlag, senior analyst at the Environmental Working Group, "Fifteen of the twenty top subsidy recipients in 2009 were primarily cotton growers. Much of these subsidies came from programs that paid based on past production, whether or not cotton was still being grown. It is a system that disproportionately benefits relatively few big growers of thirsty, chemical-dependent crops while failing to address the environmental challenges facing California agriculture."[12]

But Congress is not only serving a few American cotton oligarchs; it has expanded its largess to support cotton growers in Brazil, as a result of a trade dispute that wound its way through the World Trade Organization (WTO) over two decades. The WTO prohibits subsidies that distort trade and hurt farmers in other countries. Brazil challenged American cotton subsidies, which encourage US growers to plant cotton even when prices are low, resulting in overproduction and even more depressed prices on the world market. In 2005 the WTO upheld Brazil's challenge, a finding which the US basically ignored. The only legal recourse open to Brazil was to impose punitive tariffs and lift patent protections on $829 million worth of US goods—including nonfarm products like cars, drugs, textiles, chemicals, electronics, movies, and music. That means Brazil would prevent American goods from entering Brazil and being sold there. Immediately, the lobbyists representing these goods went to work on Congress, and between August 2009 and April 2010, the government swung into action. Rather than cut the $3 billion in cotton subsidies they pay to twenty thousand cotton growers in the US, our congressmen added to the subsidy tab by offering $150 million in "technical assistance" money to Brazilian cotton growers from the US government's export-guarantee program.[13]

That means "We the People" are paying Brazilian cotton farmers to produce cotton for the sole purpose of enabling ourselves to continue to have the privilege of paying American cotton farmers to produce cotton, too. Then, when these "mega-producers" of cotton flood the market, the global price goes down and growers in poor countries lose money on their cotton crops while the US and Brazilian growers walk away with a decent profit because US taxpayers are covering the difference between the price set by commodity markets and the actual price in the real world. It's difficult to understand because it doesn't make any sense.

This example of the true cost of growing commodities like cotton or other crops is indirect and not included in most data. Farmers will not tell you they get subsidies; the trade groups are quiet about them and the subsidies are not articulated as part of the cash receipts on a farm's income.

Not all subsidies have such dubious effectiveness: the Environmental Quality Incentives Program (EQIP), California's largest agricultural conservation program, is a subsidy designed to actually help farmers reduce pesticide use and promote conservation techniques. However, more than four thousand farmers and ranchers who sought funding from EQIP in 2009 were turned away because of a lack of funds. That program is in jeopardy of being cut further in the future.

V.

The human costs associated with food production are not recognized as actual costs at all.
Only 20 percent of California farm workers are permanent employees, and so labor is cheap for the farmers, but consumer-citizens are paying for the true cost of these workers. Farm workers live in such a state of fear and ignorance that 70 percent don't even know if they are permanent or temporary. In the 2005 National Agricultural Workers Survey, farm workers were found not to use any of the needs-based services, like MediCal, available to them through contributions from their paychecks. The most frequently used benefit was unemployment, and only 37 percent use it.[14] Though this may look like tax savings, the consumer/taxpayer will ultimately pay for the welfare of these workers, indirectly. When medical care is deferred, health issues compound and require more care and more expense, and emergency room visits are not a substitute for regular healthcare. Besides increased insurance premiums to cover expenses incurred by hospitals, hidden costs include taxes to cover increased government expenses; support of the nonprofits that help workers; and support of the legal system that processes immigration issues, deportations, and border patrols.

Relatively few farm labor contractors or direct-hire growers pay for nonmandatory benefits. Growers provide slightly more benefits than do the farm labor contractors, but, for example, only 14 percent of stone-fruit growers and 7 percent of raisin grape growers pay bonuses in the Fresno area. Transportation is provided by around 10 percent of the growers and less than a third of the growers and contractors offer housing.

A nurse in a northern California ICU described to me a controversial patient on her unit. An undocumented worker was harvesting almonds near Dixon when a piece of heavy machinery fell on him, leaving him a quadriplegic. He was airlifted to the ICU, and his brother was contacted and on hand at the unit, but he did not speak English. The staff at the hospital was angry and resentful that they had to care for this man, because he was not a citizen and had no private health insurance. Legally, he did have access to MediCal, and workers' compensation, but it is not clear that anyone at the hospital even knew that. No one at the hospital really knew what to do with him.

Someone finally contacted California Rural Legal Assistance

> ONE OF THE GREATEST NORTH AMERICAN FLYWAYS for millions of migrating birds has been stripped of trees, creeks, ponds, and marshland to form endless square miles of industrial agriculture.

(CRLA), a critical nonprofit that provides legal services to low-income Californians, the vast majority of whom are farm workers. CRLA is partially funded by community organizations, banks, law firms, and private foundations, as well as government grants from such agencies as the Department of Housing and Urban Development and the California Environmental Protection Agency. The money that funds this nonprofit travels from the pockets of California consumers to corporations who either donate directly for tax benefits or create foundations with their profits.

A young legal intern contacted the injured farm worker's brother. Beyond informing him of the patient's rights, she helped him understand that a representative of the grower would very likely appear and ask his brother to sign a release that would absolve the grower of any legal responsibility. She explained the consequences of signing that release, which might be accompanied by a small payout to the family that would never cover the lost wages resulting from the accident or the lifetime of care he would now need. Under the best of circumstances the future for a quadriplegic is severely compromised. But this is a man who cannot speak English, probably did not complete high school or even middle school, and does not have any savings or ability to secure an income. What will happen to this man? Who will pay for his care for the rest of his life? Will the US government ship him back to Mexico? The final irony is that almonds are raised in California for a global market and only 30 percent of the harvest is sold domestically. We are subsidizing the cost of production for the farmer, who sells most of his almonds abroad and pockets the profits for his own private use. Sadly, the blame for the failure of the labor system is thrown back upon the worker: what can he expect since he was illegal? He shouldn't have been here anyway. It's an attitude that perpetuates the dehumanizing views of the Jim Crow era.

VI.

Humans have not been the only casualty of agriculture. The land and formerly wild rivers flowing into the Great Central Valley have been subdued to a sterile, vast factory floor. Fields have been leveled by lasers to conform better to the GPS-guided machines that troll them. Birds and animals have been robbed of their habitats and must drink from and forage in irrigation ditches. One of the greatest North American flyways for millions of migrating birds has been stripped of trees, creeks, ponds, and marshland to form endless square miles of industrial agriculture. The valley's air is dangerously polluted by ammonia and hydrogen sulfide from massive "poop lagoons" created by industrial dairies.

Of all the environmental struggles, the biggest and most publicized problem concerns the Sacramento–San Joaquin Delta, the most important waterway in California. It is an eleven-hundred-square-mile region formed by the confluence of the San Joaquin and Sacramento rivers that connects these waters to the San Francisco Bay. In the Delta, freshwater from the mountain rivers meets salt water from the Pacific Ocean. Because of climate change, sea levels are rising and threatening to turn the Delta into a salty marsh, contaminating all that freshwater and flooding the homes and farms of Delta residents. But the salinity of the Delta is already increasing because people are siphoning water from the Sacramento River for urban and agricultural use to the degree that the Delta smelt, a bellwether of the health of the waterway, is threatened as a species. Farmers and agricultural industrialists claim that opponents of this process, primarily in the Bay Area and Los Angeles, think that the Delta smelt is more important than providing employment for workers and growing food.

Three San Joaquin farmers (Stewart & Jasper Orchards, Arroyo Farms, LLC, and King Pistachio Grove) are working a case through the courts that argues that the federal government cannot use the Endangered Species Act on the behalf of the smelt. They claim that under the US Constitution's Commerce Clause, federal agencies have no power to protect the smelt, which they say has no commercial value. The defendants in the case argue that the Endangered Species Act does not only protect commercially valued species, and who's to say that the Delta smelt may not hold some untapped commercial value? (It has been used as a baitfish and is food for the striped bass, a big sport fishing species.) These "stewards of the land" seem to be taking a very narrow and short-term view of this bellwether species: not only will their businesses be affected if the waterway is allowed to be destroyed, but their own way of life will be compromised as well.

Westlands and large growers are working hard in Washington with legislators to pass a bill, characterized as a money saver, that would overturn limits on the pumping that reverses the flow of water in two south Delta channels; eliminate requirements to allow more water to flow into the San Francisco Bay to flush salt from the Delta; and prohibit the completion of a settlement intended to restore water flows to the San Joaquin River.[15]

Essentially, this course of action would cannibalize a source of water that twenty million Californians rely on and severely impact the quality of life for the entire region—all this in exchange for short-term profits. If extinction of one species after another is what it takes to keep the earth producing at this feverish pitch, don't we need to stop and think about what we have collectively wrought? The health of the Delta smelt is directly related to the health and prosperity of farms. The choice is whether to allow the Delta to continue to become more salty and the Delta smelt to go the way of the dodo bird, or to make a stand and try to preserve the environment as it is now. If we ignore the increased salinity of the Delta water, the farmers who use that salty Delta water will face decreased crop yields anyway. Excessive water exports are not only harmful to the Sacramento–San Joaquin Delta's ecosystems but have a negative impact on the public health and commercial lives of local residents. The continued depletion of

IF EXTINCTION OF ONE SPECIES AFTER ANOTHER is what it takes to keep the earth producing at this feverish pitch, don't we need to stop and think about what we have collectively wrought?

freshwater will result in reduced water quality for Delta residents, forcing the need for additional treatment of local drinking water. If a plan is put into place to preserve the normal salinity of the Delta, then growers will have to either find more efficient ways to use water or get it elsewhere. Getting water elsewhere is an enormous challenge fraught with still more controversy, environmental issues, and cost. There is really no easy answer now.

Meanwhile, land deep in the valley which receives the diverted water is also becoming saltier as a byproduct of irrigation on that clay soil. The result of not finding a balance now for the ecosystem is that not only will we lose the Delta smelt (and other fish, like the coho salmon that are threatened by water exports from the Russian River) as a food source, but also we will render vast tracts of land unusable for food production and suffer the attendant job loss along the economic spectrum. It is a lose-lose scenario, but the logic of the arguments is buried under emotional and partisan ideals.

While a great deal of environmental damage is considered collateral to farming, the valley is also the disposal site of choice for toxic materials from all over the state because the residents there have no real political or economic power. In Kettleman City, the middle of this important farmland, lies the largest toxic dump west of Alabama. For decades all manner of toxic substances have been brought to the other two toxic dumps in the valley and to Kettleman—a place thought not to be in anyone's backyard, except for the fifteen hundred Latino farm workers who began living there after the California Aqueduct was built in the 1970s. Last year the Kettleman site, owned by Waste Management, accepted 356,000 tons of hazardous waste, consisting of tens of thousands of chemical compounds, including asbestos, pesticides, caustics, petroleum products, and 11,000 tons of material contaminated with PCBs, known carcinogens. A great deal of this came from the coastal consumers who have outlawed the storage of toxins in their own neighborhoods.

These poisons have been accumulating and seeping into the earth right next to farmland and the California Aqueduct, despite numerous orders by the EPA to clean up the site, the most recent in July 2010. Plans are underway to dump 500,000 tons a year of sewage sludge from Los Angeles there as well.[16] A hornet's nest of politics and old-school leadership has kept cleanup efforts at bay. Meanwhile local supervisors enjoy the nearly $2 million paid by Waste Management in franchise and property taxes each year. The landfill is monitored, regulated, and controlled by nearly a dozen state and federal agencies. In the twenty-eight years of its operation, the company has been fined over $2 million for infractions, including mishandling of PCBs, failing to properly analyze incoming wastes, stormwater, and leachate for PCBs, and failing to properly calibrate equipment.[17] The community of farm workers has recently experienced a marked increased in birth defects. The site continues to operate its business as usual with the same old promises to make changes in the future.

FARM WORKER Madera County, California, 2007

SMOG, FEEDLOT, AND VALLEY MOUNTAINS Cottonwood, California, 2007

POLLINATION Dos Palos, California, 2005

TOMATOES, 50¢ A BUCKET Madera, California, 2008

"PEST CONTROL" BILLBOARD   Highway 33, California, 2007

NEW FRUIT TREES Highway 198, Huron, California, 2006

FIELD WORKER West Valley, San Joaquin Valley, California, 2008

ORCHARD REMOVAL Tulare County, California, 2008

POWER LINES AND ORCHARD Highway 180, Central Valley, California, 2006

AERIAL APPLICATORS "Helping to provide safe food for America's tables." Tulare, California, 2008

SPRAYING PESTICIDE Patterson, California, 2007

CARLOS, 14, AND ESTEVAN, 12 "Comida sin pesticidas"/Food without pesticides, Plainview, California, 2007

THE SAN JOAQUIN VALLEY Tulare, California, 2008

SPRAYING MUTICIDE 80 gallons per load, Merced, California, 2010

ASTHMA Francisco Martinez, Plainview, California, 2006

TEAPOT DOME DUMP Refuse disposal site, Tulare, California, 2007

EMMANUEL AND HIS MOTHER Born with cleft lip and seizures near a toxic waste dump, Kettleman City, California, 2010

INDUSTRIAL DAIRY, 94°F Tulare County, California, 2007

"PROTECT YOUR FISH" California Aqueduct, San Joaquin Valley, California, 2008

CAMPESINO Migrant trailer camp, Mendota, California, 2006

MIGRANT WORKER Trailer camp, Mendota, California, 2006

HANDS OF AN ASPARAGUS PICKER Madera County, California, 2007

PULL-UPS Woodlake, California, 2008

YOLANDA AND MARK ANTHONY Trailer #12, Mendota, California, 2006

RAFAEL "Fear of God," Madera, California, 2008

PAULA GALLEGO, 79 YEARS OLD St. Andrews Mission, Tonyville, California, 2007

CHRISTMAS POSADA St. Andrews Mission, Tonyville, California, 2007

CHRIST Mendota, California, 2009

MADONNA Sunday service, Dos Palos, California, 2007

CEMETERY Merced, California, 2008

"50 CENT" Asparagus picker, Madera, California, 2007

VII.

A poisoned, straightjacketed land-scape, resource mismanagement, glaring human rights abuses, and the hijacking of our democracy to form an agricultural oligarchy are not only a source of shame for Americans but the ingredients for disaster. The window for actually making changes in the way we conduct business is closing. Biology and science are nonnegotiable. There is a tipping point, and it is not something that will allow for our government to operate as usual with its mashup of special interest initiatives that result in the compromise of principles. This is a critical time for people to come together and work toward the higher purpose of preserving life on the planet. But we must do more than turn back the amount of carbon spewing into the air. We must admit ignorance and defeat about the entire cycle of development. Not only is it not right to create wealth on the backs of the world's poor, it is uneconomical. We must see that short-term profits and wealth are drained away later when society must shore up a dysfunctional and ever-growing swath of humanity. Until the way to wealth is softened with some modicum of compassion and responsibility toward not only the workers but toward the earth, the cycle will persist. We must look up the food chain and demand accountability from business owners.

The definition of one's tribe has to be enlarged beyond "my family," "my company," "my race," "my economic class" to include humanity, plants, and animals of the world's ecosystems. That's a big leap and a lot to ask of people who feel it is their right to pursue their personal empires. Whatever happened to our country's motto, "Out of many, one"?

California growers are well educated and open to diversifying their portfolios. They have been on the cutting edge of new technology for decades. Let us not forget, California farmers invented industrial farming, and some of the best technology, and now, urban planning practices for urban/rural development are coming out of Silicon Valley. The grave challenges we face collectively are not lost

THE AGRICULTURAL COMMUNITY IS CAPABLE OF TURNING THEIR IMMENSE POLITICAL AND ECONOMIC POWER TO MEET SOCIAL AND ENVIRONMENTAL CHALLENGES. THE REAL QUESTION IS WHETHER THEY WILL DO ENOUGH ON A LARGE ENOUGH SCALE BEFORE THE COST OF REMEDIATING THE ENVIRONMENT BECOMES PROHIBITIVE.

on them and when it is profitable to act, they do, as is demonstrated by applications to build two massive solar farms, one in the Mojave Desert and one in the valley's Kern County.[18] A few dairy ranchers have invested in dairy manure digesters which convert methane, a byproduct of cow manure, into electricity or natural gas, thus reducing greenhouse gas emissions created by the release of methane into the air and eliminating the seepage of nitrates from dairy manure into the groundwater. Clearly, the agricultural community is capable of turning their immense political and economic power to meet social and environmental challenges. The real question is whether they will do enough on a large enough scale before the cost of remediating the environment becomes prohibitive.

By now, the picture painted here might seem bleak and psychic numbing may be setting in. We invite you to resist that feeling and to channel your energy into action, no matter how small. Both valley residents and coastal folk can enter an expanded sphere of awareness. It is easy to live in ignorance about the true cost of our lifestyles and food sources on the coast, just as it is easy to feel isolated and cut off from the coast as a valley resident. We need to build connections, starting with the most simple and basic sort. Shop at a farmer's market, and try to arrange for a family field trip to the farm that is growing your food. Ask your host to give you a tour of the neighboring farm communities. If you're from the coastal regions, the next time you are speeding through the valley, budget in an hour to drive away from the truck stops and away from the AM/PM Mini Market. Drive into the tiny farm towns. Don't be afraid to talk to the waitress at the burrito shop. And then think about it. Is this right? Is it okay? Hopefully, this will excite you to seek out answers for yourself. There are many organizations working on these problems from many different angles all across the state, and you can easily gather a variety of approaches and points of view that might differ or contradict each other. Ask questions and channel the answers to change the course of a system that is headed toward self-destruction.

WE NEED TO BUILD CONNECTIONS, starting with the most simple and basic sort. Shop at a farmer's market, and try to arrange for a family field trip to the farm that is growing your food.

New ideas have to make sense and people must be persistent in making a case for change. The awkward, autistic Temple Grandin convinced beef ranchers that it was more efficient, more profitable, and yes, more humane to revamp the process by which cows are slaughtered. She was so passionate and persistent that ranchers had to listen eventually. It took her a long time but there is a new understanding of how cattle behave, and a new awareness that when cows are not stressed or anxious and, at least, look happy, the whole operation works better. Now over half of all slaughterhouses in the US use her protocols. When enough people persistently push back, a lot of change can happen very quickly.

In the end, there is really no one else to whom we can appeal for help. In a democracy there is no authority supervising our activities, or correcting or preventing our mistakes. Each of us must participate and influence the outcomes of today's challenges and live with the results. History describes to us our foibles and our potential to reach glory, so we know both the depths and heights the human story spans. It is easier to sink with gravity, but how deliciously proud we can be when we achieve the heights.

GRAPE PICKER, "SARK'S SUNSHINE FRESH" Sanger, California, 2006

RANCH ALTAR Highway 140, San Joaquin Valley, California, 2008

FARM WORKER Mendota, California, 2009

OLD CARS, FAULDER RANCH Highway 140, San Joaquin Valley, California, 2008

GUADALUPE, 26-YEAR-OLD MOTHER OF FIVE WHO HAD HER FIRST CHILD AT 14 San Joaquin, California, 2009

ORCHARD REMOVAL, FANTOZZI FARMS Patterson, California, 2006

STOPPED DEVELOPMENT Atwater, California, 2006

FORECLOSED Moving day, Cynthia, 7 years old, Merced, California, 2008

WOODSIDE HOMES DEVELOPMENT Tulare, California, 2007

136

SOUTH LAKE TAHOE DRIVE Chowchilla, California, 2008

OIL DERRICK IN ORCHARD Dickenson, California, 2008

PRAYING Trailer camp, Mendota, California, 2006

ORANGE PICKERS Tulare, California, 2007

BIRDS Tulare County, California, 2007

CALIFORNIA AQUEDUCT San Joaquin Valley, California, 2008

ABANDONED SUBDIVISION Tulare County, California, 2008

DOS PALOS ROAD Firebaugh, California, 2009

NOTES

1. "California Agricultural Production Statistics 2009–2010," California Department of Food and Agriculture, 2011, http://www.cdfa.ca.gov/statistics.

2. "Texas Ag Stats," Texas Department of Agriculture, 2006, http://www.agr.state.tx.us/agr/main_render/0,1968,1848_37142_0_0,00.html?channelId=37142.

3. Jeff Onsted, "Farming on the Fringe: Can Tax Incentives Save California's Farmlands?" *Next American City* 11 (Summer 2006), http://americancity.org/magazine/article/farming-on-the-fringe-onstead.

4. Arundhati Roy, *The Cost of Living* (New York: Modern Library, 1999), p. 15.

5. "Increasing Food Security among Agricultural Workers in the Salinas Valley of California," US Dept. of Agriculture REEIS, 2010, http://www.reeis.usda.gov/web/crisprojectpages/218065.html.

6. "2011 Farm Subsidy Database, Environmental Working Group, accessed June 29, 2011, http://farm.ewg.org/top_recips.php?fips=00000&progcode=total.

7. Susan Sward, "Farmers Fear Loss of Tax Breaks—and Land," *The Bay Citizen,* last updated July 14, 2010, www.baycitizen.org/development/story/farmers-fear-loss-tax-breaks/.

8. "Farm Workers' Rights, 70 Years Overdue." *New York Times,* April 5, 2009.

9. "California's Agricultural Employment," Employment Development Department, 2008, http://www.calmis.ca.gov/file/agric/ca-ag-profile.pdf.

10. "Labor Laws for Farmworkers," *Farmworker Justice,* accessed June 29, 2011, www.fwjustice.org/us-labor-law-for-farmworkers.

11. "California Cotton Grows to over 300,000 Acres," Sierra2TheSea, December 11, 2010, www.sierra2thesea.com/sierra2thesea.com/Home/Entries/2010/12/11_California_Cotton_GrowsTo_Over_300,000_Acres.html.

12. Kari Hamerschlag, "Farm Subsidies in California: Skewed Priorities and Gross Inequities," accessed June 29, 2011, http://farm.ewg.org/pdf/california-farm.pdf.

13. Michael Grunwald, "Why the U.S. Is Also Giving Brazilians Farm Subsidies," time.com, April 9, 2010, www.time.com/time/nation/article/0,8599,1978963,00.html.

14. Sabrina J. Isé, Jeffrey M. Perloff, Steve R. Sutter, and Suzanne Vaupel, "Directly Hiring Workers versus Using Farm Labor Contractors," University of California Agricultural Personnel Management Program Publication APMP003.

15. Mike Taugher, "GOP Targets Water Rules," *Contra Costa Times,* February 15, 2011.

16. Jacques Leslie, "What's Killing the Babies of Kettleman City?" *Mother Jones* (July/August, 2010), pp. 50–54.

17. Louis Sahagun, "Toxic Waste Dump Receives New EPA Order to Clean Up Contaminated Soil," *Los Angeles Times,* July 17, 2010, http://articles.latimes.com/2010/jul/17/local/la-me-toxic-20100717.

18. Todd Woody, "California Approves First New U.S. Thermal Solar Plant," *New York Times Green* blog, August 25, 2010, http://green.blogs.nytimes.com/2010/08/25/california-approves-first-u-s-thermal-solar-plant/?src=mv.

BIBLIOGRAPHY

Arax, Mark, and Rick Wartzman. *The King of California: J. G. Boswell and the Making of a Secret American Empire.* New York: PublicAffairs, 2003.

Barlow, Maude. *Blue Covenant: The Global Water Crisis and the Coming Battle for the Right to Water.* New York: The New Press, 2008.

Haslam, Gerald. *The Other California: The Great Central Valley in Life and Letters.* Reno: Univ. of Nevada Press, 1990.

Johnson, Stephen, Gerald Haslam, and Robert Dawson. *The Great Central Valley: California's Heartland.* Berkeley: University of California Press, 1993.

Kimbrell, Andrew, ed. *Fatal Harvest: The Tragedy of Industrial Agriculture.* Washington, D.C.: Island Press, 2002.

Kotkin, Joel, and Paul Grabowicz. *California, Inc.* New York: Rawson, Wade Publishers, 1982.

Light, Ken. *With These Hands.* New York: Pilgrim Press, 1986.

Mayfield, Thomas Jefferson. *Indian Summer: Traditional Life among the Choinumne Indians of California's Central Valley.* Berkeley: Heyday Books, 1993.

McWilliams, Carey. *Factories in the Field: The Story of Migratory Farm Labor in California.* Boston: Little, Brown and Co., 1939.

Reisner, Marc. *Cadillac Desert: The American West and Its Disappearing Water.* New York: Viking, 1986.

Roy, Arundhati. *The Cost of Living.* New York: Modern Library, 1999.

Shell, Ellen Ruppel. *Cheap: The High Cost of Discount Culture.* New York: The Penguin Press, 2009.

Starr, Kevin. *Endangered Dreams The Great Depression in California.* New York: Oxford University Press, 1996.

———. *Coast of Dreams: California on the Edge, 1990–2003.* New York: Alfred A. Knopf, 2004.

———. *California: A History.* New York: Modern Library, 2007

Taylor, Ronald B. *Sweatshops in the Sun: Child Labor on the Farm.* Boston: Beacon Press, 1973.

Yogi, Stan, ed. *Highway 99: A Literary Journey through California's Great Central Valley.* Berkeley: Heyday Books, 1996.

ACKNOWLEDGMENTS

Looking back at our notes, we realize that this book belongs to many along the road who offered financial support, directions, contacts, and their thoughts about the communities that were photographed and the issues that were examined in the San Joaquin Valley. So many generously gave their time to this project, one has the realization that it does take many hands to create a book.

When we met with Ben Jealous in 2006, then newly appointed president of the Rosenberg Foundation, to discuss our new project about the Great Central Valley in California we never expected to receive support, but we did. That seed money started a rich, complicated search to make sense of that sprawling, mighty land and its amazing peoples. We also have Ellen Widess, also at the Rosenberg Foundation at that time, to thank for support for this project.

The generosity of Suzie Katz and PhotoWings, Peter Buckley, Stewart Davidson, and Joyce Linker supported this book. They all stepped forward and helped Heyday make it happen. As we struggled to help fund this book, dear Topher Delaney acted as a guiding angel and cheerleader. Her love for telling the story of the valley's people and its land sustained us with the energy to not give up the good fight!

Ken's assistants and interns worked tirelessly, without complaint, and unselfishly gave of themselves to the photographic parts of this work. Chris Tompkins and Sabrina Wong offered early help with Photoshop and scanning. Dan Figueroa spent months faithfully cleaning dust and dirt from all the digital scans, and Maxwell Cohen spent years making many of the silver prints from the project in the wet darkroom. Dashel Moore joined as an assistant near the end of the project and helped in the last weeks of work. Joshua Partridge offered advice and help with the cover image. Uri Korn oversaw the creation of the digital files with good conversation and thoughtful advice. Erika Gentry rode in during the final weeks of image preparation without a moment's hesitation, and with mastery, amazing technical knowledge, and calming advice, took the digital files and completed the final images for publication with Ken. All of them kept Ken company during the gestation of the photographs. Mark Liebman of Pictopia generously made his facility available for the creation of digital exhibition prints.

As the text began to take form, several friends and colleagues were kind enough to take the time to thoughtfully read and offer feedback to Melanie. Her deeply felt gratitude goes to Inez Hollander Lake, Dorothy Moore, and Dierdre English.

Photographer Michael Light offered to take Ken up in his two-seater airplane, and winged him over the valley, sharing his extensive picture-taking experience and friendship. Sandra Phillips, senior curator at the San Francisco Museum of Modern Art, and Erin O'Toole, assistant curator, took a stab at the sequencing of the images and opened Ken's eyes to seeing them in new ways.

Ken's colleagues at Newsweek.com, director of photography Kathy Jones, picture editor Margaret (Maggie) Keady, and reporter Katie Paul, sent him into the valley on assignment and then created a powerful multimedia piece using the images. It was a finalist in the National Magazine Awards and had a spectacular 2.5 million page turns. Wayne and Joan Miller looked at early photos and offered encouragement. Jeffrey Smith of Contact Press Images had thoughtful ideas about getting the individual images out into the world.

Originally, Melanie hoped to include bits from the forty-plus interviews she made with a huge variety of people living in the valley. A round of thanks to Laurie Burkitt, Rob Krieger, Ellen Chen, Amy Jeffries, Lisa Rowland, and Sean Aronson for their good work meticulously transcribing them. Ananda Shorey became Melanie's go-to transcriber not only because of her great work and great translations from Spanish, but for her enthusiasm for this project. In the end, we did not use the interviews much at all, though all the time and effort people spent describing their lives and perspectives have been internalized and are at the root of the words in this book.

Many people pointed us in the right direction and told us stories, using their personal connections to help us see the valley so that the words and pictures would be better informed. Of the many people in the valley with whom Melanie spoke, who trusted her with their personal stories and who love the valley and want it to thrive, here are a few that should be acknowledged for sharing themselves with her: Jim Taubert, Rick Cosyns, Janie Gatzman, Jess Ponce, Yolanda Prada, Angel Huerta, Ron Fantozzi, Kevin Donlon, Annalisa Sanchez, Joe Freitas, Piedad Ayala, Sharon Wakefield, and the Water Marchers in Mendota. A very special note of appreciation goes to Elfie and Maia Ballis, who spent a great deal of time speaking with her when Elfie was very, very ill. Their lives were dedicated to creating social and environmental justice in the valley and, though Elfie has since passed away, his legacy will live on.

Ken extends his appreciation to Lydia Gutierrez of Fresno Catholic Charities, who gave good advice. Her husband, Mark Gutierrez, volunteered his time to take him out to the homeless camps in Fresno. Many community organizers translated and opened doors: Irma Medellin, Irma Arrollo, Elva Beltran, Vincente Gomez, Anita Martinez, Irma Barazza, Melissa Barazza, Pastor Rafael Marquez, Guadalupa Nune, Sister Libby Fernandez, and Joan Burke of Loaves and Fishes. Others, in governmental positions or the media, were helpful as well: Alma Martinez of Radio Bilingüe, photographer Victor Blue, Mendota mayor Robert Silva, chief civil deputy Mike Motz, elementary school principal Randy DeGraw, and Mendota Westside Youth Center founder Nancy Daniels. All of them allowed us inside their worlds. Francisco Barazza spent a great deal of time with both Melanie and Ken, sharing his world, his family, and his passionate drive to improve life in the valley.

We are honored to have Thomas Steinbeck contribute his wonderful words and history of the valley to this book. Thom's, partner, Gail Knight, expressed enthusiasm and support that meant a great deal to us both. A debt of gratitude goes to Malcolm Margolin, who took a blind leap of faith to do this book and then stood by the results, and to Gayle Wattawa, not only a terrific editor but a great midwife to the birth of this book. We thank production editor Diane Lee for her deft touch and the excellent staff at Heyday who have all put their hearts into producing a book of which both of us feel extraordinarily proud. Thanks to Lorraine Rath for her beautiful design and Natalie Mulford, Heyday marketing director, for her efforts to reach the whole nation with this book.

Though Melanie came home with the idea of exploring the valley as a joint project, it was Ken who forged ahead and overcame the many challenges this book presented. While Melanie juggled this project and her job, Ken very patiently absorbed her vision and moved the project forward for both of them. She offers her deepest debt of gratitude and highest admiration to Ken for believing that this is an important voice to bring to the table. Truly, if it were not for his dogged persistence, this work would never have been completed, published, or shown in public.

Ken offers this dedication, "for my Muse and wife Melanie, whose sharp wit sensed an important story and urged me to go into the valley and photograph. During my four years of travels I carried a scribbled note I found wrapped in a sandwich on an early trip. It read, 'Dearest Ken—may the wind be to your back and the light ever beautiful as you explore and travel for our project.' These images would not have been created, nor would this book, without her vision and love. In times of struggle around this project she supported me and lived with my frustrations and energy. Thank You!"

152

ABOUT THE AUTHORS

MELANIE LIGHT is a writer whose most recent book is *Coal Hollow*. She has published two special edition books, *Night at the Met* with photographs by Larry Fink and *Mad Day Out* with photos of the Beatles. She is the cofounding executive director of Fotovision, a nonprofit dedicated to supporting the international community of documentary photographers, and is the recipient of grants from the Soros Documentary Fund and the Rosenberg Foundation. She teaches and lectures internationally.

KEN LIGHT is an internationally recognized social documentary photographer and recipient of two NEA photography fellowships. The author of eight books, including *Delta Time, Coal Hollow, To the Promised Land, Texas Death Row*, and *Witness in Our Time,* he is also a full-time faculty member and director of the Center for Photography at the Graduate School of Journalism at the University of California, Berkeley, and a Laventhol visiting professor at Columbia University.

HEYDAY
into California

About Heyday

Heyday is an independent, nonprofit publisher and unique cultural institution. We promote widespread awareness and celebration of California's many cultures, landscapes, and boundary-breaking ideas. Through our well-crafted books, public events, and innovative outreach programs we are building a vibrant community of readers, writers, and thinkers.

Thank You

It takes the collective effort of many to create a thriving literary culture. We are thankful to all the thoughtful people we have the privilege to engage with. Cheers to our writers, artists, editors, storytellers, designers, printers, bookstores, critics, cultural organizations, readers, and book lovers everywhere!

We are especially grateful for the generous funding we've received for our publications and programs during the past year from foundations and hundreds of individual donors. Major supporters include:

Anonymous; Evenor Armington Fund, James Baechle; Bay Tree Fund; B.C.W. Trust III; S. D. Bechtel, Jr. Foundation; Barbara Jean and Fred Berensmeier; Berkeley Civic Arts Program and Civic Arts Commission; Joan Berman; Peter and Mimi Buckley; Lewis and Sheana Butler; California Council for the Humanities; California Indian Heritage Center Foundation; California State Library; California Wildlife Foundation/California Oak Foundation; Keith Campbell Foundation; Candelaria Foundation; John and Nancy Cassidy Family Foundation, through Silicon Valley Community Foundation; Center for California Studies; The Christensen Fund; The City of Berkeley; Compton Foundation; Lawrence Crooks; Nik Dehejia; George and Kathleen Diskant; Donald and Janice Elliott, in honor of David Elliott, through Silicon Valley Community Foundation; Euclid Fund at the East Bay Community Foundation; Eustace-Kwan Charitable Fund; Federated Indians of Graton Rancheria; Mark and Tracy Ferron; Judith Flanders; Furthur Foundation; The Fred Gellert Family Foundation; Wallace Alexander Gerbode Foundation; Wanda Lee Graves and Stephen Duscha; Alice Guild; Walter & Elise Haas Fund; Coke and James Hallowell; Hawaii & Sons; Carla Hills; Sandra and Chuck Hobson; G. Scott Hong Charitable Trust; James Irvine Foundation; JiJi Foundation; Kendeda Fund; Marty and Pamela Krasney; Guy Lampard and Suzanne Badenhoop; LEF Foundation; Judy McAfee; Michael McCone; Joyce Milligan; Moore Family Foundation; National

Endowment for the Arts; National Park Service; Theresa Park; Patagonia, Inc., Pease Family Fund, in honor of Bruce Kelley; The Philanthropic Collaborative; Philanthropic Ventures Foundation; PhotoWings; Alan Rosenus; Rosie the Riveter/WWII Home Front NHP; The San Francisco Foundation; San Manuel Band of Mission Indians; Savory Thymes; Hans Schoepflin; Contee and Maggie Seely; Martha Stanley; Stanley Smith Horticultural Trust; William Somerville; Stone Soup Fresno; James B. Swinerton; Swinerton Family Fund; Thendara Foundation; Tides Foundation; TomKat Charitable Trust; Lisa Van Cleef and Mark Gunson; Marion Weber, Whole Systems Foundation; John Wiley & Sons; Peter Booth Wiley and Valerie Barth; Dean Witter Foundation; and Yocha Dehe Wintun Nation.

Board of Directors

Getting Involved

To learn more about our publications, events, membership club, and other ways you can participate, please visit www.heydaybooks.com.